TO LIVE IN HIS LOVE
I LIVE TO PLEASE HIM
BOOK 2

By Elizabeth C. (Betsy) Tice

DEDICATION

This devotional is dedicated to family and friends who desire a deeper understanding of living in the presence of the Lord.

<u>This is book TWO of a two-part series, but may also be read as a stand-alone.</u>

Conformed to His Image

By Elizabeth C. (Betsy) Tice

THE INSPIRATION

GALATIANS 4:19 My little children, of whom I travail in birth again until Christ be formed in you,

GALATIANS 2:10 Only they would that we should remember the poor; the same which I also was forward to do.

ACTS 9:15 But the Lord said unto him, Go thy way: for he is a chosen vessel unto me, to bear my name before the Gentiles, and kings, and the children of Israel:

MATTHEW 5:16 Let your light so shine

before men, that they may see your good works, and glorify your Father which is in heaven.

Conformed to His Image
****** SONG **********
By Elizabeth C. (Betsy) Tice
(Galatians 4:19, Galatians 2:10, Acts 9:15, and Matthew 5:16)

CHORUS:

Conformed to His image.

That is the goal.

Yielded completely,

beneath His control.

Glorify Jesus, with all I am.

Laying my life down to find it again.

VERSE:

A chosen vessel I long to be.
The light of Your presence

shine forth through me.

Glorify Jesus, with all I am.

Laying my life down to find it again.

CHORUS:

Conformed to His image.

That is the goal.

Yielded completely,

beneath His control.

Glorify Jesus, with all I am.

Laying my life down to find it again.

Am I Serving Jesus

By Elizabeth C. (Betsy) Tice

THE INSPIRATION

Acts 9:5 And he said, Who art thou, Lord? And the Lord said, I am Jesus whom thou persecutest: *it is* hard for thee to kick against the pricks.

Mathew 5:16 Let your light so shine before men, that they may see your good works, and glorify your Father which is in heaven.

2 Corinthians 5:10 For we must all appear before the judgment seat of Christ; that every one may receive the things *done* in *his* body, according to that he hath done, whether *it be* good or bad.

John 16:2 They shall put you out of the synagogues: yea, the time cometh, that whosoever killeth you will think that he doeth God service.

Am I Serving Jesus

********** SONG **********

 By Elizabeth C. (Betsy) Tice

(Acts 9, especially verse 5, Matthew 5:16, II Corinthians 5:10, and John 16:2)

 CHORUS:

"Am I serving Jesus?"

is all I need to ask.

"Am I serving Jesus?"

no matter what the task.

VERSE:

Lord, a chosen vessel for You

I long to be.

The light of Your dear presence

shine forth for all to see.

CHORUS:

"Am I serving Jesus?"

is all I need to ask.

"Am I serving Jesus?"

no matter what the task.

He's Waiting To Hear From His Sheep

By Elizabeth C. (Betsy) Tice

THE INSPIRATION

Psalm 121:4 Behold, he that keepeth Israel shall neither slumber nor sleep.

Matthew 11:28-29 Come unto me, all *ye* that labour and are heavy laden, and I will give you rest. 29 Take my yoke upon you, and learn of me; for I am meek and lowly in heart: and ye shall find rest unto your souls. Psalm 62:8 Trust in him at all times; *ye* people, pour out your heart before him: God *is* a refuge for us. Selah.

1 Peter 5:7 Casting all your care upon him; for he careth for you.

Revelation 3:20 Behold, I stand at the door, and knock: if any man hear my voice, and open the door, I will come in to him, and will sup with him, and he with me.

Revelation 5:8 And when he had taken the book, the four beasts and four *and* twenty elders fell down before the Lamb, having every one of them harps, and golden vials full of odours, which are the prayers of saints.

He's Waiting To Hear From His Sheep

********** SONG **********

By Elizabeth C. (Betsy) Tice

(Psalm 121:4, Matthew 11:28-29, Psalm 62:8, I Peter 5:7, Rev. 3:20, and Rev. 5:8)

CHORUS 1:

The God of Israel does not slumber.

The God of Israel never sleeps.

So pour out your heartaches unto Him.

He's waiting to hear from His sheep.

VERSE 1:

Sometimes the road seems so lonely, and feelings inside make you weep;

But Jesus is calling unto you,

"I gave My life for My sheep."
CHORUS 2:
Yes, Jesus is waiting to hear you,
for you are one of His sheep.
Your prayers are to Him
like sweet perfume.
His thoughts are to you very deep.
VERSE 2:
"Behold I stand at the door…
of your heart.
Oh, My child, can't you hear?
Just open the door to My Spirit.
For you know,
Perfect love casts out fear."
CHORUS 3:
"Yes, I am waiting to hear you,
for you are one of My sheep.

Your prayers are to Me like sweet perfume.

My thoughts are to you of great peace."

VERSE 3:

"Come unto Me, to the weary.

Come unto Me, to the weak.

Don't carry your burden any longer.

It's you I came here to seek."

CHORUS 3   CHORUS 1

 CHORUS

"SEEK MY FACE"

"Seek My face. Seek My face.

If you would partake of my grace.

Seek My face. Seek My face.

The answer will come,

When you seek My face."

"I'm waiting to hear from My sheep."

SPECIAL NOTE

"I Am Your Lamb" represents a response to the words of "He's Waiting To Hear from His Sheep," another song that the Holy Spirit gave me to write. As I read the Scriptures underneath the title, I was particularly impressed and inspired by the words in John where we read that He calls His sheep by name. He doesn't just call, "Here, sheep!" We are all special and beloved to Him. What a thought!

I Am Your Lamb

By Elizabeth C. (Betsy) Tice

THE INSPIRATION

Psalm 23 1The LORD *is* my shepherd; I shall not want. 2 He maketh me to lie down in green pastures: he leadeth me beside the still waters. 3 He restoreth my soul: he leadeth me in the paths of righteousness for his name's sake. 4 Yea, though I walk through the valley of the shadow of death, I will fear no evil: for thou *art* with me; thy rod and thy staff they comfort me. 5 Thou preparest a table before me in the presence of mine enemies: thou anointest my head with oil; my cup runneth over. 6 Surely goodness and mercy shall follow me all the days of my life: and I will dwell in the house of the LORD for ever.

John 10:1 – 18 Verily, verily, I say unto you, He that entereth not by the door into the sheepfold, but climbeth up some other way, the same is a thief and a robber. 2 But he that entereth in by the door is the shepherd of the sheep. 3 To him the porter openeth; and the sheep hear his voice: and he calleth his own sheep by name, and leadeth them out. 4 And when he putteth forth his own sheep, he goeth before them, and the sheep follow him: for they know his voice. 5 And a stranger will they not follow, but will flee from him: for they know not the voice of strangers. 6 This parable spake Jesus unto them: but they understood not what things they were which he spake unto them. 7 Then said Jesus unto them again, Verily, verily, I say unto you, I am the door of the sheep. 8 All that ever came before me are thieves and robbers: but the sheep did not hear them. 9 I am the door: by me if any man enter in, he shall be saved, and shall go in and out, and find pasture. 10 The thief cometh not, but for to steal, and to kill, and to destroy: I am come that they might have life, and that they might have *it* more abundantly. 11 I am the good shepherd: the good shepherd giveth his life for the sheep. 12 But he that is an hireling, and not the shepherd, whose own the sheep are not, seeth the wolf coming, and leaveth the sheep, and fleeth: and the wolf catcheth them, and scattereth the sheep. 13 The hireling fleeth, because he is an hireling, and careth not for the sheep. 14 I am the good shepherd, and know my *sheep,* and am known of mine. 15 As the Father knoweth me, even so know I the Father: and I lay down my life for the sheep. 16 And other sheep I have, which are not of this fold: them also I must bring, and they shall hear my voice; and there shall be one fold, *and* one shepherd. 17 Therefore doth my Father love me, because I lay down my life, that I might take it again. 18 No man taketh it from me, but I lay it down of myself. I have power to lay it down, and I have power to take it again. This commandment have I received of my Father.

Revelation 22:20 – 21 He which testifieth these things saith, Surely I come quickly. Amen. Even so, come, Lord Jesus. 21 The grace of our Lord Jesus Christ *be* with you all. Amen.

I Am Your Lamb

********** SONG **********

By Elizabeth C. (Betsy) Tice

(Psalm 23, John 10:1 – 18, and

Revelation 22:20 – 21)

CHORUS:

I am Your lamb. I am Your lamb.

By waters gently feeding,

I am Your lamb.

VERSE 1:

Safe in Your arms. Safe in Your arms.

Safe in Your arms I'm carried.

Safe in Your arms.

VERSE 2:

Safe from all harm. Safe from all harm.

Abiding in Your Shadow,

Safe from all harm.

VERSE 3:

Saved by Your blood.

Saved by Your blood.

Saved from the grip of satan,

Saved by your blood.

VERSE 4:

Wounded for me.

Wounded for me.

Healed by the stripes You bore,

Wounded for me.

VERSE 5:

You know my name.

You know my name.

I am Your special pet lamb.

You know my name.

VERSE 6:

I hear Your voice.

I hear Your voice.

I follow You, my shepherd.

I hear Your voice.

VERSE 7:

I love You so. I love You so.

You are my Lord and Master.

I love You so.

VERSE 8:

Waiting for me.

Waiting for me.

Seated in Heav'n exalted,

Waiting for me.

VERSE 9:

Coming for me.

Coming for me.

Even so, come Lord Jesus.

Coming for me.

CHORUS:

I am Your lamb.

I am Your lamb.

By waters gently feeding,

I am Your lamb.

Peter, Do You Love Me

By Elizabeth C. (Betsy) Tice

THE INSPIRATION

John 21:15-17 So when they had dined,

Jesus saith to Simon Peter, Simon, *son* of Jonas, lovest thou me more than these? He saith unto him, Yea, Lord; thou knowest that I love thee. He saith unto him, Feed my lambs. 16 He saith to him again the second time, Simon, *son* of Jonas, lovest thou me? He saith unto him, Yea, Lord; thou knowest that I love thee. He saith unto him, Feed my sheep. 17 He saith unto him the third time, Simon, *son* of Jonas, lovest thou me? Peter was grieved because he said unto him the third time, Lovest thou me? And he said unto him, Lord, thou knowest all things; thou knowest that I love thee. Jesus saith unto him, Feed my sheep.

John 14:21-26 He that hath my commandments, and keepeth them, he it is that loveth me: and he that loveth me shall be loved of my Father, and I will love him, and will manifest myself to him. 22 Judas saith unto him, not Iscariot, Lord, how is it that thou wilt manifest thyself unto us, and not unto the world? 23 Jesus answered and said unto him, If a man love me, he will keep my words: and my Father will love him, and we will come unto him, and make our abode with him. 24 He that loveth me not keepeth not my sayings: and the word which ye hear is not mine, but the Father's which sent me. 25 These things have I spoken unto you, being *yet* present with you. 26 But the Comforter, *which is* the Holy Ghost, whom the Father will send in my name, he shall teach you all things, and bring all things to your remembrance, whatsoever I have said unto you.

Matthew 7:21-27 Not every one that saith unto me, Lord, Lord, shall enter into the kingdom of heaven; but he that doeth the will of my Father which is in heaven. 22 Many will say to me in that day, Lord, Lord, have we not prophesied in thy name? and in thy name have cast out devils? and in thy name done many wonderful works? 23 And then will I profess unto them, I never knew you: depart from me, ye that work iniquity. 24 Therefore whosoever heareth these sayings of mine, and doeth them, I will liken him unto a wise man, which built his house upon a rock: 25 And the rain descended, and the floods came, and the winds blew, and beat upon that house; and it fell not: for it was founded upon a rock.

26 And every one that heareth these sayings of mine, and doeth them not, shall be likened unto a foolish man, which built his house upon the sand: 27 And the rain descended, and the floods came, and the winds blew, and beat upon that house; and it fell: and great was the fall of it.

Peter, Do You Love Me

********** SONG **********

By Elizabeth C. (Betsy) Tice

(John 21:15-16 and Matthew 7:21-23)

VERSE 1:

"Peter, do you love me?"

"Yes, my Lord."

"Peter, do you love me?"

"Yes, my Lord."

"Feed My lambs. Feed My sheep.

If you truly love Me, feed my sheep."

VERSE 2:

"Preacher, do you love me?"

"Yes, my Lord."

"Preacher, do you love me?"

"Yes, my Lord."

"Feed My lambs. Feed My sheep.

If you truly love Me, feed my sheep."

VERSE 3:

"Christian, do you love me?"

"Yes, my Lord."

"Christian, do you love me?"

"Yes, my Lord."

"Do the things that I say.

If you truly love Me, you'll obey."

As a Child

By Elizabeth C. (Betsy) Tice

THE INSPIRATION

Matthew 18:1 – 5 At the same time came the disciples unto Jesus, saying, Who is the greatest in the kingdom of heaven? 2 And Jesus called a little child unto him, and set him in the midst of them, 3 And said, Verily I say unto you, Except ye be converted, and become as little children, ye shall not enter into the kingdom of heaven. 4 Whosoever therefore shall humble himself as this little child, the same is greatest in the kingdom of heaven. 5 And whoso shall receive one such little child in my name receiveth me.

Proverbs 3:5 – 6 Trust in the LORD with all thine heart; and lean not unto thine own understanding. 6 In all thy ways acknowledge him, and he shall direct thy paths.

James 1:17 Every good gift and every perfect gift is from above, and cometh down from the Father of lights, with whom is no variableness, neither shadow of turning.

Matthew 7:10-11 Or if he ask a fish, will he give him a serpent? 11 If ye then, being evil, know how to give good gifts unto your children, how much more shall your Father which is in heaven give good things to them that ask him?

Luke 12:32 Fear not, little flock; for it is your Father's good pleasure to give you the kingdom.

As a Child

********** SONG **********

By Elizabeth C. (Betsy) Tice

(Matthew 18:1 – 5, Proverbs 3:5 – 6, James 1:17, Matthew 7:10, and Luke 12:32)

CHORUS:

As a child our Heav'nly

Father's calling us to be.

Trust in Him with all our hearts

until His dear face we shall see.

VERSE 1:

We can fully trust our Father,

for He loves us so.

He sent His only Son to save

us while we were in sin here below.

VERSE 2:

Life and love and joy and peace

are what the Father gives.
We must then be subject to
the Father of spirits and live.
VERSE 3:
If we ask of Him a fish,
will He a serpent give?
No, He gives good gifts unto us
That we might abundantly live.
CHORUS:
As a child our Heavn'ly
Father's calling us to be.
Trust in Him with all our hearts
until His dear face we shall see.

Humble Yourselves

By Elizabeth C. (Betsy) Tice

THE INSPIRATION

1 Peter 5:6 Humble yourselves therefore under the mighty hand of God, that he may exalt you in due time:

Hebrews 10:35-36 Cast not away therefore your confidence, which hath great recompence of reward. 36 For ye have need of patience, that, after ye have done the will of God, ye might receive the promise.

Revelation 1:7 Behold, he cometh with clouds; and every eye shall see him, and they *also* which pierced him: and all kindreds of the earth shall wail because of him. Even so, Amen.

Revelation 22:12-13 And, behold, I come quickly; and my reward *is* with me, to give every man according as his work shall be. 13 I am Alpha and Omega, the beginning and the end, the first and the last.

Matthew 24:27 For as the lightning cometh out of the east, and shineth even unto the west; so shall also the coming of the Son of man be.

Humble Yourselves

********** SONG **********

By Elizabeth C. (Betsy) Tice

(Based on I Peter 5:6, Hebrews 10:35-6,
Revelation 1:7; 22:12-13, Matthew 24:27)

CHORUS:

Humble yourselves. Humble yourselves.

Humble yourselves

Under the mighty hand of God,

under the mighty hand of God,

And He will exalt you. (X3)

in His time.

VERSE 1:

Cast not away your confidence. (X3)

Which has a great reward.

For soon our Lord will come,

Will come in clouds of glory.

The Alpha and Omega will
split the eastern sky.
CHORUS 2:
Behold I come. Behold I come.
Behold I come.
And behold, I come quickly,
And My reward is with me
To give to every man according
as his work shall be.
CHORUS:
Humble yourselves. Humble yourselves.
Humble yourselves
Under the mighty hand of God,
under the mighty hand of God,
And He will exalt you.
And He will exalt you.
And He will exalt you In His time.

Christ in You, the Hope of Glory

By Elizabeth C. (Betsy) Tice

THE INSPIRATION

John 14:12 Verily, verily, I say unto you, He that believeth on me, the works that I do shall he do also; and greater *works* than these shall he do; because I go unto my Father.

John 3:16-17 For God so loved the world, that he gave his only begotten Son, that whosoever believeth in him should not perish, but have everlasting life. 17 For God sent not his Son into the world to condemn the world; but that the world through him might be saved.

Colossians 1:27 To whom God would make known what *is* the riches of the glory of this mystery among the Gentiles; which is Christ in you, the hope of glory:

Matthew 10:7-8 And as ye go, preach, saying, The kingdom of heaven is at hand. 8 Heal the sick, cleanse the lepers, raise the dead, cast out devils: freely ye have received, freely give.

John 16:33 These things I have spoken unto you, that in me ye might have peace. In the world ye shall have tribulation: but be of good cheer; I have overcome the world.

Philippians 2:11-13 And *that* every tongue should confess that Jesus Christ *is* Lord, to the glory of God the Father. 12 Wherefore, my beloved, as ye have always obeyed, not as in my presence only, but now much more in my absence, work out your own salvation with fear and trembling. 13 For it is God which worketh in you both to will and to do of *his* good pleasure.

Christ in You,
the Hope of Glory
********** SONG **********

By Elizabeth C. (Betsy) Tice

(John 14:12, John 3:16-17, Col.1:27, Matthew 10:7-8, John 16:33, and Philippians 2:11-13)

CHORUS:

Christ in you, the hope of glory.

Tell to all the wondrous story.

Christ in you, the hope of glory,

Who salvation brought.

VERSE 1:

Christ in you, the hope of glory.

Tell to all the wondrous story.

Christ in you, the hope of glory.
Heals and makes men whole.

VERSE 2:
Christ in you, the hope of glory.
Tell to all the wondrous story.
Christ in you, the hope of glory.
Sets the captives free.
VERSE 3:
Christ in you said, "Be of good cheer.
You have nothing left to fear.
In the world, there's tribulation.
But I have overcome."

CHORUS:

Christ in you, the hope of glory.

Tell to all the wondrous story.

Christ in you, the hope of glory,

Who salvation brought.

I Won't Share
My Glory

By Elizabeth C. (Betsy) Tice and
Bishop O.L. (Ty) Tice

THE INSPIRATION

Isaiah 42:8 I am the LORD: that is my name: and my glory will I not give to another, neither my praise to graven images.

Isaiah 45:22 Look unto me, and be ye saved, all the ends of the earth: for I *am* God, and *there is* none else.

Exodus15:26 And said, If thou wilt diligently hearken to the voice of the LORD thy God, and wilt do that which is right in his sight, and wilt give ear to his commandments, and keep all his statutes, I will put none of these diseases upon thee, which I have brought upon the Egyptians: for I *am* the LORD that healeth thee.

Titus 2:14 Who gave himself for us, that he might redeem us from all iniquity, and purify unto himself a peculiar people, zealous of good works.

Isaiah 1:18-19 Come now, and let us reason together, saith the LORD: though your sins be as scarlet, they shall be as white as snow; though they be red like crimson, they shall be as wool. 19 If ye be willing and obedient, ye shall eat the good of the land:

Acts 12:22-23 And immediately the angel of the Lord smote him, because he gave not God the glory: and he was eaten of worms, and gave up the ghost. 24 But the word of God grew and multiplied.

I Won't Share My Glory

********** SONG **********

By Elizabeth C. (Betsy) Tice and
 Bishop O.L. (Ty) Tice
(Isaiah 42:8, Isaiah 45:22, Exodus15:26, Titus 2:14, Isaiah 1:18-19, and Acts 12:22-23)

CHORUS:

I won't share My glory.

I won't share My glory.

I won't share My glory with any man.

VERSE 1:

I will do the saving.

I will do the healing.

I will do the cleansing.

Just call out to Me.

CHORUS:

I won't share My glory.

I won't share My glory.

I won't share My glory with any man.

It's God Who Gave You Your Gift

By Elizabeth C. (Betsy) Tice

THE INSPIRATION

1 Corinthians 4:1-7 Let a man so account of us, as of the ministers of Christ, and stewards of the mysteries of God. 2 Moreover it is required in stewards, that a man be found faithful. 3 But with me it is a very small thing that I should be judged of you, or of man's judgment: yea, I judge not mine own self. 4 For I know nothing by myself; yet am I not hereby justified: but he that judgeth me is the Lord. 5 Therefore judge nothing before the time, until the Lord come, who both will bring to light the hidden things of darkness, and will make manifest the counsels of the hearts: and then shall every man have praise of God. 6 And these things, brethren, I have in a figure

transferred to myself and *to* Apollos for your sakes; that ye might learn in us not to think *of men* above that which is written, that no one of you be puffed up for one against another. 7 For who maketh thee to differ *from another?* and what hast thou that thou didst not receive? now if thou didst receive *it,* why dost thou glory, as if thou hadst not received *it?*

1 Corinthians 12 1-31 Now concerning spiritual *gifts,* brethren, I would not have you ignorant. 2 Ye know that ye were Gentiles, carried away unto these dumb idols, even as ye were led. 3 Wherefore I give you to understand, that no man speaking by the Spirit of God calleth Jesus accursed: and *that* no man can say that Jesus is the Lord, but by the Holy Ghost. 4 Now there are diversities of gifts, but the same Spirit. 5 And there are differences of administrations, but the same Lord. 6 And there are diversities of operations, but it is the same God which worketh all in all. 7

But the manifestation of the Spirit is given to every man to profit withal. 8 For to one is given by the Spirit the word of wisdom; to another the word of knowledge by the same Spirit; 9 To another faith by the same Spirit; to another the gifts of healing by the same Spirit; 10 To another the working of miracles; to another prophecy; to another discerning of spirits; to another *divers* kinds of tongues; to another the interpretation of tongues: 11 But all these worketh that one and the selfsame Spirit, dividing to every man severally as he will. 12 For as the body is one, and hath many members, and all the members of that one body, being many, are one body: so also *is* Christ. 13 For by one Spirit are we all baptized into one body, whether *we be* Jews or Gentiles, whether *we be* bond or free; and have been all made to drink into one Spirit. 14 For the body is not one member, but many. 15 If the foot shall say, Because I am not the hand, I am not of the body; is it therefore not of the body? 16

And if the ear shall say, Because I am not the eye, I am not of the body; is it therefore not of the body? 17 If the whole body *were* an eye, where *were* the hearing? If the whole *were* hearing, where *were* the smelling? 18 But now hath God set the members every one of them in the body, as it hath pleased him. 19 And if they were all one member, where *were* the body? 20 But now *are they* many members, yet but one body. 21 And the eye cannot say unto the hand, I have no need of thee: nor again the head to the feet, I have no need of you. 22 Nay, much more those members of the body, which seem to be more feeble, are necessary: 23 And those *members* of the body, which we think to be less honourable, upon these we bestow more abundant honour; and our uncomely *parts* have more abundant comeliness. 24 For our comely *parts* have no need: but God hath tempered the body together, having given more abundant honour to that *part* which lacked: 25 That there should be no schism in the body; but *that* the members should have the same care one for another. 26 And whether one member suffer, all the members suffer with it; or one member be honoured, all the members rejoice with it. 27 Now ye are the body of Christ, and members in particular. 28 And God hath set some in the church, first apostles, secondarily prophets, thirdly teachers, after that miracles, then gifts of healings, helps, governments, diversities of tongues. 29 *Are* all apostles? *are* all prophets? *are* all teachers? *are* all workers of miracles? 30 Have all the gifts of healing? do all speak with tongues? do all interpret? 31 But covet earnestly the best gifts: and yet shew I unto you a more excellent way.

It's God Who Gave
You Your Gift

********** SONG **********

By Elizabeth C. (Betsy) Tice

(I Cor.4:1-7 and I Cor. 12)

VERSE 1:

 "Puff, puff, puff, puff."

"It's God Who gave you your gift!

REPEAT 3 TIMES

So, you better glory in the Lord."

VERSE 2:

"I am an eye."

"It's God Who gave you your gift!"

"I am a hand."

"It's God Who gave you your gift!"

"I am a foot."

"It's God Who gave you your gift! So,
you better glorify His name!"

VERSE 3:

"I am so wise."

"It's God Who gave you your gift."

"I have all faith."

"It's God Who gave you your gift."

"I speak in tongues."

"It's God Who gave you your gift

So, you better stop and praise the Lord!"

VERSE 4:

"So, don't pretend it's yours
 cuz you were so great,

And for the praise,

you'd best for the judgment day wait.

Our glass is dark, and God has the final say,

So, you better leave it up to him."

VERSE 5:

"Praise, praise, praise, praise.

It's God, and He is so great!

REPEAT 3 TIMES

So, we'll glorify the Lord of Lords.

So, we'll glorify the Lord of Lords." (X2)

Stir up the Gift

By Elizabeth C. (Betsy) Tice

THE INSPIRATION

2 Timothy 1:6-7 Wherefore I put thee in remembrance that thou stir up the gift of God, which is in thee by the putting on of my hands. 7 For God hath not given us the spirit of fear; but of power, and of love, and of a sound mind.

James 5:16-20 Confess *your* faults one to another, and pray one for another, that ye may be healed. The effectual fervent prayer of a righteous man availeth much. 17 Elias was a man subject to like passions as we are, and he prayed earnestly that it might not rain: and it rained not on the earth by the space of three years and six months. 18 And he prayed again, and the heaven gave rain, and the earth brought forth her fruit. 19 Brethren, if any of you do err from the truth, and one convert him; 20 Let him know, that he which converteth the sinner from the error of his way shall save a soul from death, and shall hide a multitude of sins.

1 John 5:14-15 And this is the confidence that we have in him, that, if we ask any thing according to his will, he heareth us: 15 And if we know that he hear us, whatsoever we ask, we know that we have the petitions that we desired of him.

Hebrews 12:1-2 Wherefore seeing we also are compassed about with so great a cloud of witnesses, let us lay aside every weight, and the sin which doth so easily beset *us,* and let us run with patience the race that is set before us, 2 Looking unto Jesus the author and finisher of *our* faith; who for the joy that was set before him endured the cross, despising the shame, and is set down at the right hand of the throne of God.

Philippians 1:6 Being confident of this very thing, that he which hath begun a good work in you will perform *it* until the day of Jesus Christ:

Stir up the Gift

********** SONG **********

By Elizabeth C. (Betsy) Tice
(II Timothy 1:6-7, James 5:16-20, I John
5:14-15, Hebrews 12:1-2. and Philippians
1:6)

CHORUS (1):
Stir, stir, stir, stir, stir, stir, stir up the gift.
His Spirit lives in you today.
He'll give you power, love,
and a sound mind,
And He will chase your fear away!

VERSE 1:

Why don't you pray the way Elijah prayed?

He told the king his words were true.

Your Word will be according to His will,

And He will hear and answer you.

VERSE 2:

Why don't you look to Jesus on the cross,

The One Who shed His blood for you?

He is the author of your "precious faith,"

And He'll complete the work in you.

CHORUS (2):

Stir, stir, stir, stir, stir, stir, stir up the gift.

God's Holy Spirit lives in you.

He'll give you power, love,

and a sound mind.

He'll give you grace to see you through.

Thank You, Jesus, for Dying for Me Medley

By Elizabeth C. (Betsy) Tice

THE INSPIRATION

1 Peter 2:24-25 Who his own self bare our sins in his own body on the tree, that we, being dead to sins, should live unto righteousness: by whose stripes ye were healed. 25 For ye were as sheep going astray; but are now returned unto the Shepherd and Bishop of your souls. Luke 24:1-8 Now upon the first *day* of the week, very early in the morning, they came unto the sepulchre, bringing the spices which they had prepared, and certain *others* with them. 2 And they found the stone rolled away from the sepulchre. 3 And they entered in, and found not the body of the Lord Jesus. 4 And it came to pass, as they were much perplexed thereabout, behold, two men stood by them in shining garments: 5 And as they were afraid, and bowed down

their faces to the earth, they said unto them, Why seek ye the living among the dead? 6 He is not here, but is risen: remember how he pake unto you when he was yet in Galilee, 7 Saying, The Son of man must be delivered into the hands of sinful men, and be crucified, and the third day rise again. 8 And they remembered his words,

Acts 1:9-11And when he had spoken these things, while they beheld, he was taken up; and a cloud received him out of their sight. 10 And while they looked stedfastly toward heaven as he went up, behold, two men stood by them in white apparel; 11 Which also said, Ye men of Galilee, why stand ye gazing up into heaven? this same Jesus, which is taken up from you into heaven, shall so come in like manner as ye have seen him go into heaven.

Revelation 22:20 He which testifieth these things saith, Surely I come quickly. Amen.

Even so, come, Lord Jesus.

Thank You, Jesus,

for Dying for Me Medley
********** SONG **********

By Elizabeth C. (Betsy) Tice
(I Peter 2:24, Luke 24:1-8, Acts 1:9-11,
and Revelation 22:20)

"Thank You, Jesus, for Dying for Me"
Thank You, Jesus, for dying for me,
Shedding Your life's blood
upon the cruel tree.
Paying the ransom that I might go free.
Thank you, Lord.

"Were You There When They Crucified My
Lord?" (A Negro Spiritual in Public
Domain)

Verse 1:

Were you there when they
crucified my Lord?
Were you there when they
crucified my Lord?
Oh! Oh! Oh! Oh!
Sometimes it causes me
to tremble, tremble, tremble.
Were you there when
they crucified my Lord?

Verse 2:

Were you there when they
nailed Him to the tree?
Were you there when they
nailed Him to the tree?
Oh! Oh! Oh! Oh!

Sometimes it causes me to
tremble, tremble, tremble.
Were you there when they
nailed Him to the tree?
Verse 3:
Were you there when the
sun refused to shine?
Were you there when the sun
refused to shine?
Oh! Oh! Oh! Oh!
Sometimes it causes me
to tremble, tremble, tremble.
Were you there when the sun
refused to shine?
Verse 4:
Were you there when they
laid Him in the tomb?

Were you there when they
laid Him in the tomb?
Oh! Oh! Oh! Oh!
Sometimes it causes me
to tremble, tremble, tremble.
Were you there when they
laid Him in the tomb?
Verse 5:
Were you there when He
rose up from the grave?
Were you there when He
rose up from the grave?
Oh! Oh! Oh! Oh!
Sometimes I feel like
shouting "Glory! Glory! Glory!"
Were you there when He
rose up from the grave?

Verse 6:
Were you there when He
ascended into Heaven?
Were you there when He
ascended into Heaven?
Oh! Oh! Oh! Oh!
Sometimes I want to say,
 "Come quickly! Quickly! Quickly!"
Were you there when He
ascended into Heaven?

A Grateful Praise

By Elizabeth C. (Betsy) Tice

THE INSPIRATION

Luke 17:11-19

11 And it came to pass, as he went to Jerusalem, that he passed through the midst of Samaria and Galilee. 2 And as he entered into a certain village, there met him ten men that were lepers, which stood afar off: 13 And they lifted up *their* voices, and said, Jesus, Master, have mercy on us. 14 And when he saw *them,* he said unto them, Go shew yourselves unto the priests. And it came to pass, that, as they went, they were cleansed. 15 And one of them, when he saw that he was healed, turned back, and with a loud voice glorified God, 16 And fell down on *his* face at his feet, giving him thanks: and he was a Samaritan.

17 And Jesus answering said, Were there not ten cleansed? but where *are* the nine? 18 There are not found that returned to give glory to God, save this stranger. 19 And he said unto him, Arise, go thy way: thy faith hath made thee whole.

A Grateful Praise

********** SONG **********

By Elizabeth C. (Betsy) Tice

(Luke 17:11-19, I Thessalonians 5:18, and 5:23 KJV)

VERSE 1:

Ten lepers came to Jesus,

Seeking mercy from the Lord.

On them He had compassion,

According to their word.

VERSE 2:

As they went away from Jesus,

Obeying what He said.

They saw that they were cleansed,

Their bodies no longer dead.

VERSE 3:

The Samaritan said, "Thank you,"

And fell at Jesus' feet.

He worshiped Him so loudly,

His healing was complete.

VERSE 4:

May I be found like the grateful stranger,

In worship at Your feet.

For only then will I be made whole,

And my joy will be complete.

Slowly with feeling:

For only then will I be made whole,

And my joy will be complete.

We Ask You Dear Jesus

By Elizabeth C. (Betsy) Tice

THE INSPIRATION

Acts 4:29-33 And now, Lord, behold their threatenings: and grant unto thy servants, that with all boldness they may speak thy word, 30 By stretching forth thine hand to heal; and that signs and wonders may be done by the name of thy holy child Jesus. 31 And when they had prayed, the place was shaken where they were assembled together; and they were all filled with the Holy Ghost, and they spake the word of God with boldness. 32 And the multitude of them that believed were of one heart and of one soul: neither said any *of them* that ought of the things which he possessed was his own; but they had all things common. 33 And with great power gave the apostles witness of the resurrection of the Lord Jesus: and great grace was upon them all.

Mark 16:15-20 And he said unto them, Go ye into all the world, and preach the gospel to every creature. 16 He that believeth and is baptized shall be saved; but he that believeth not shall be damned. 17 And these signs shall follow them that believe; In my name shall they cast out devils; they shall speak with new tongues; 18 They shall take up serpents; and if they drink any deadly thing, it shall not hurt them; they shall lay hands on the sick, and they shall recover. 19 So then after the Lord had spoken unto them, he was received up into heaven, and sat on the right hand of God. 20 And they went forth, and preached every where, the Lord working with *them,* and confirming the word with signs following. Amen.

John 21:25 And there are also many other things which Jesus did, the which, if they should be written every one, I suppose that even the world itself could not contain the books that should be written. Amen.

We Ask You Dear Jesus

********** SONG **********

By Elizabeth C. (Betsy) Tice

(Matthew 28:18-20, Revelation 22:20)

CHORUS

Do it again, Lord. Do it again.

Stretch forth Your hand to

the children of men.

Grant signs and wonders

in Your Holy Name.

We ask You, Dear Jesus, do it again.

VERSE 1

We read in the gospels how

You walked among men.
Healed the sick, raised the dead,
 again and again,
So many works the books could not contain.
Then You went up to Heaven
and gave us Your Name.

CHORUS
Do it again, Lord. Do it again.
Stretch forth Your hand to
the children of men.
Grant signs and wonders
in Your Holy Name.
We ask You, Dear Jesus, do it again.

Declare and See
What the Lord Has Done

By Elizabeth C. (Betsy) Tice

THE INSPIRATION

Acts 14:3 Long time therefore abode they speaking boldly in the Lord, which gave testimony unto the word of his grace, and granted signs and wonders to be done by their hands.

Acts 14:27 And when they were come, and had gathered the church together, they rehearsed all that God had done with them, and how he had opened the door of faith unto the Gentiles.

Revelation 12:11 And they overcame him by the blood of the Lamb, and by the word of their testimony; and they loved not their lives unto the death.

Psalm 34:8 O taste and see that the LORD is good: blessed is the man that trusteth in him.

Declare and See
What the Lord Has Done
********** SONG **********

By Elizabeth C. (Betsy) Tice

(Acts 14:3, Acts 14:27, Revelation 12:11, and Psalm 34:8)

VERSE 1:

Declare and see what the Lord has done.

Declare and see what the Lord has done.

Declare and see what the Lord has done.

And He will do it again.

VERSE 2:

"They overcame by the blood of the Lamb.

They overcame by the blood of the Lamb.

They overcame by the blood of the Lamb

And by the Word of their witness."

VERSE 3:

"We overcome by the blood of the Lamb.

We overcome by the blood of the Lamb.

We overcome by the blood of the Lamb

And by the Word of our witness."

VERSE 4:

"Oh, taste and see that the Lord is good. Oh, taste and see that the Lord is good.

Oh, taste and see that the Lord is good." His love is forevermore.

Die to Self; Bring Forth Fruit

By Elizabeth C. (Betsy) Tice

THE INSPIRATION

John 12:24 Verily, verily, I say unto you, Except a corn of wheat fall into the ground and die, it abideth alone: but if it die, it bringeth forth much fruit.

Die to Self; Bring Forth Fruit

********** SONG **********

By Elizabeth C. (Betsy) Tice

(John 12:24 KJV)

CHORUS:

Except a corn of wheat die to self,

It abideth alone.

Except a corn of wheat die to self,

It abideth alone.

VERSE 1:

But if it dies, it brings forth fruit,

Much fruit for the Kingdom of God.

But if it dies, it brings forth fruit,

Much fruit for the Kingdom of God.

VERSE 2:

Oh, Jesus, help me die to self.
Let me live out my life for You,
That in death or life, lived by Your design,
I'll bring glory to the Kingdom of God.

Take Thy Cross and Follow Me

By Elizabeth C. (Betsy) Tice

THE INSPIRATION

John 12:27-36 Now is my soul troubled; and what shall I say? Father, save me from this hour: but for this cause came I unto this hour. 28 Father, glorify thy name. Then came there a voice from heaven, *saying,* I have both glorified *it,* and will glorify *it* again. 29 The people therefore, that stood by, and heard *it,* said that it thundered: others said, An angel spake to him. 30 Jesus answered and said, This voice came not because of me, but for your sakes. 31 Now is the judgment of this world: now shall the prince of this world be cast out. 32 And I, if I be lifted up from the earth, will draw all *men* unto me. 33 This he said, signifying what death he should die. 34 The people answered him, We have heard out of the law that Christ abideth for ever: and how sayest thou, The Son of man must be lifted up?

who is this Son of man? 35 Then Jesus said unto them, Yet a little while is the light with you. Walk while ye have the light, lest darkness come upon you: for he that walketh in darkness knoweth not whither he goeth. 36 While ye have light, believe in the light, that ye may be the children of light. These things spake Jesus, and departed, and did hide himself from them.

John 21:18-22 Verily, verily, I say unto thee, When thou wast young, thou girdedst thyself, and walkedst whither thou wouldest: but when thou shalt be old, thou shalt stretch forth thy hands, and another shall gird thee, and carry *thee* whither thou wouldest not. 19 This spake he, signifying by what death he should glorify God. And when he had spoken this, he saith unto him, Follow me. 20 Then Peter, turning about, seeth the disciple whom Jesus loved following; which also leaned on his breast at supper, and said, Lord, which is he that betrayeth thee? 21 Peter seeing him saith to Jesus, Lord, and what *shall* this man *do?* 22 Jesus saith unto him, If I will that he tarry till I come, what *is that* to thee? follow thou me.

Matthew 16:24-25 Then said Jesus unto his disciples, If any *man* will come after me, let him deny himself, and take up his cross, and follow me. 25 For whosoever will save his life shall lose it: and whosoever will lose his life for my sake shall find it.

Take Thy Cross
and Follow Me
********** SONG **********

By Elizabeth C. (Betsy) Tice
(John 12:32-33, John 21:18-22, and
Matthew 16:24-25 KJV)

CHORUS:
If I will that he should tarry,
what is that to thee?
If I will that he should tarry,
take thy cross and follow Me.
VERSE 1:
Long ago, the Savior called

to Peter by the sea.

Long ago, He said unto him,

"Leave thy nets and follow Me."

VERSE 2:

Can't you hear the Savior calling,

calling unto thee?

Can't you hear Him say unto you,

"Take thy cross and follow Me?"

VERSE 3:

He who saves his life shall lose it.

He who seeks shall surely find.

He who loses life shall find it.

For his life is hid in Mine.

CHORUS:

If I will that he should tarry,

what is that to thee?

If I will that he should tarry,

take thy cross and follow Me.

A Horse, a Horse is a Vain Thing for Safety

By Elizabeth C. (Betsy) Tice

THE INSPIRATION

Psalm 33:17 An horse *is* a vain thing for safety: neither shall he deliver *any* by his great strength.

Ephesians 6:11-17 Put on the whole armour of God, that ye may be able to stand against the wiles of the devil. 12 For we wrestle not against flesh and blood, but against principalities, against powers, against the rulers of the darkness of this world, against spiritual wickedness in high *places*. 13 Wherefore take unto you the whole armour of God, that ye may be able to withstand in the evil day, and having done all, to stand. 14 Stand therefore, having your loins girt about with truth, and having on the breastplate of righteousness; 15 And your feet shod with the preparation of the gospel of peace; 16 Above all, taking the shield of faith, wherewith ye shall be able to quench all the fiery darts of the wicked. 17 And take the helmet of salvation, and the sword of the Spirit, which is the word of God:

 I Peter 2:24 Who his own self bare our sins in his own body on the tree, that we, being dead to sins, should live unto righteousness: by whose stripes ye were healed.

A Horse, a Horse
is a Vain Thing for Safety
********** SONG **********

By Elizabeth C. (Betsy) Tice

(Psalm 33:17, Ephesians 6:11-17, and I Peter 2:24)

CHORUS:

A horse, a horse is a vain thing for safety.

I will not fear. What can man do to me?

A horse, a horse is a vain thing for safety.

I trust in God. He'll deliver me.

VERSE 1:

So if you're looking to get into battle,

Don't put your trust in the things you can see.

Just wear the armor of God for protection.

For you're a child of the King, you see.

VERSE 2:

Oh, Hallelu, Hallelujah to Jesus,

The one who died on Calvary's tree.

Oh, Hallelu, Hallelujah to Jesus.

His precious blood has made me free.

CHORUS:

A horse, a horse is a vain thing for safety.

I will not fear. What can man do to me?

A horse, a horse is a vain thing for safety.

I trust in God. He'll deliver me.

LAST TIME- I trust in God.

He'll deliver me. (X3)

The Jonah Song

By Elizabeth C. (Betsy) Tice

THE INSPIRATION

Jonah Chapters 1,2,3

Jonah 1:1 Now the word of the LORD came unto Jonah the son of Amittai, saying, 2 Arise, go to Nineveh, that great city, and cry against it; for their wickedness is come up before me. 3 But Jonah rose up to flee unto Tarshish from the presence of the LORD, and went down to Joppa; and he found a ship going to Tarshish: so he paid the fare thereof, and went down into it, to go with them unto Tarshish from the presence of the LORD. 4 But the LORD sent out a great wind into the sea, and there was a mighty tempest in the sea, so that the ship was like to be broken. 5 Then the mariners were afraid, and cried every man unto his god, and cast forth the wares that *were* in the ship into the sea, to lighten *it* of them. But Jonah was gone down into the sides of the ship; and he lay, and was fast asleep. 6 So the shipmaster came to him, and said unto him, What meanest thou, O sleeper? arise, call upon thy God, if so be that God will think upon us, that we perish not. 7 And they said every one to his fellow, Come, and let us cast lots, that we may know for whose cause this evil *is* upon us. So they cast lots, and the lot fell upon Jonah. 8 Then said they unto him, Tell us, we pray thee, for whose cause this evil *is* upon us; What *is* thine occupation? and whence comest thou? what *is* thy country? and of what people *art* thou? 9 And he said unto them, I *am* an Hebrew; and I fear the LORD, the God of heaven, which hath made the sea and the dry *land.* 10 Then were the men exceedingly afraid, and said unto him, Why hast thou done this?

For the men knew that he fled from the presence of the LORD, because he had told them. 11 Then said they unto him, What shall we do unto thee, that the sea may be calm unto us? for the sea wrought, and was tempestuous. 12 And he said unto them, Take me up, and cast me forth into the sea; so shall the sea be calm unto you: for I know that for my sake this great tempest *is* upon you. 13 Nevertheless the men rowed hard to bring *it* to the land; but they could not: for the sea wrought, and was tempestuous against them. 14 Wherefore they cried unto the LORD, and said, We beseech thee, O LORD, we beseech thee, let us not perish for this man's life, and lay not upon us innocent blood: for thou, O LORD, hast done as it pleased thee. 15 So they took up Jonah, and cast him forth into the sea: and the sea ceased from her raging. 16 Then the men feared the LORD exceedingly, and offered a sacrifice unto the LORD, and made vows. 17 Now the LORD had prepared a great fish to swallow up Jonah. And Jonah was in the belly of the fish three days and three nights.

Jonah 2:1-10 Then Jonah prayed unto the LORD his God out of the fish's belly, 2 And said, I cried by reason of mine affliction unto the LORD, and he heard me; out of the belly of hell cried I, *and* thou heardest my voice. 3 For thou hadst cast me into the deep, in the midst of the seas; and the floods compassed me about: all thy billows and thy waves passed over me. 4 Then I said, I am cast out of thy sight; yet I will look again toward thy holy temple. 5 The waters compassed me about, *even* to the soul: the depth closed me round about, the weeds were wrapped about my head. 6 I went down to the bottoms of the mountains; the earth with her bars *was* about me for ever: yet hast thou brought up my life from corruption, O LORD my God. 7 When my soul fainted within me I remembered the LORD: and my prayer came in unto thee, into thine holy temple. 8 They that observe lying vanities forsake their own mercy. 9 But I will sacrifice unto thee with the voice of thanksgiving; I will pay *that* that I have vowed. Salvation *is* of the LORD. 10 And the LORD spake unto the fish, and it vomited out Jonah upon the dry *land.*

Jonah 3:1-10 And the word of the LORD came unto Jonah the second time, saying, 2 Arise, go unto Nineveh, that great city, and preach unto it the preaching that I bid thee. 3 So Jonah arose, and went unto Nineveh, according to the word of the LORD. Now Nineveh was an exceeding great city of three days' journey. 4 And Jonah began to enter into the city a day's journey, and he cried, and said, Yet forty days, and Nineveh shall be overthrown. 5 So the people of Nineveh believed God, and proclaimed a fast, and put on sackcloth, from the greatest of them even to the least of them. 6 For word came unto the king of Nineveh, and he arose from his throne, and he laid his robe from him, and covered *him* with sackcloth, and sat in ashes. 7 And he caused *it* to be proclaimed and published through Nineveh by the decree of the king and his nobles, saying, Let neither man nor beast, herd nor flock, taste any thing: let them not feed, nor drink water: 8 But let man and beast be covered with sackcloth, and cry mightily unto God: yea, let them turn every one from his evil way, and from the violence that *is* in their hands. 9 Who can tell *if* God will turn and repent, and turn away from his fierce anger, that we perish not? 10 And God saw their works, that they turned from their evil way; and God repented of the evil, that he had said that he would do unto them; and he did *it* not.

The Jonah Song

********** SONG **********

By Elizabeth C. (Betsy) Tice

(The book of Jonah)

VERSE 1:

"Oh, Lord, You know, You know,

I don't wanna' go.

Oh, Lord, You know, You know,

I don't wanna' go.

Oh, Lord, You know, You know,

I don't wanna' go.

'cuz I'm in my comfort zone."

VERSE 2:

"Oh, Lord, You know, You know,

I'm in the belly of the fish.

Oh, Lord, You know, You know,

I'm in the belly of the fish.

Oh, Lord, You know, You know,

I'm in the belly of the fish.

Please make him spit me out."

Jonah replies, "Thanks. I needed that!"

God calls Jonah again to go to Ninevah and preach a message of repentance.

VERSE 3:

"Oh, Lord, I'll go,

I'll go where you want me to go.

Oh, Lord, I'll do,

I'll do what you want me to do.

Oh, Lord, I'll say,

I'll say what you want me to say,

'cuz my eyes are fixed on You."

I Don't Wanna' Stay Here,
Safe in the Boat

(Peter's Song)

By Elizabeth C. (Betsy) Tice

THE INSPIRATION

Matthew 14:22-33 And straightway Jesus constrained his disciples to get into a ship, and to go before him unto the other side, while he sent the multitudes away. 23 And when he had sent the multitudes away, he went up into a mountain apart to pray: and when the evening was come, he was there alone. 24 But the ship was now in the midst of the sea, tossed with waves: for the wind was contrary. 25 And in the fourth watch of the night Jesus went unto them, walking on the sea. 26 And when the disciples saw him walking on the sea, they were troubled, saying, It is a spirit; and they cried out for fear. 27 But straightway Jesus spake unto them, saying, Be of good cheer; it is I; be not afraid. 28 And Peter answered him and said, Lord, if it be thou, bid me come unto thee on the water. 29 And he said, Come. And when Peter was come down out of the ship, he walked on the water, to go to Jesus. 30 But when he saw the wind boisterous, he was afraid; and beginning to sink, he cried, saying, Lord, save me. 31 And immediately Jesus stretched forth *his* hand, and caught him, and said unto him, O thou of little faith, wherefore didst thou doubt? 32 And when they were come into the ship, the wind ceased. 33 Then they that were in the ship came and worshipped him, saying, Of a truth thou art the Son of God.

I Don't Wanna' Stay Here, Safe in the Boat

********** SONG **********

By Elizabeth C. (Betsy) Tice

(Based on Matthew 14:22-33)

(Peter's Song)

CHORUS:

I don't wanna' stay here safe in the boat.

I wanna' walk on the water with my Jesus.

I don't wanna' stay here safe in the boat.

I wanna' walk on the water with my Jesus.

BRIDGE 1:

Bid me come, Lord. Bid me come, Lord.

Bid me come, Lord, to Your side.

Bid me come, Lord. Bid me come, Lord.

Bid me come, Lord, walk with You.

VERSE 1:

Satan is a liar, and he's under my feet,

'cuz I'm walking on the water

with my Jesus.

My foot is on his neck,

and my joy is complete,

'cuz I'm walking on the water

with my Jesus.

BRIDGE 2:

See, I'm walking. See, I'm walking.

See, I'm walking with my Lord. (Repeat)
CHORUS 2:

I don't wanna' stay here safe in the boat.

I wanna' dance on the water with my Jesus.

I don't wanna' stay here safe in the boat.

I wanna' dance on the water with my Jesus.
BRIDGE 2:

Bid me come, Lord. Bid me come, Lord.

Bid me come, Lord, dance with You.

Bid me come, Lord. Bid me come, Lord.

Bid me come, Lord, dance with You.

VERSE 2:

Satan is a liar, and he's under my feet,

'cuz I'm dancing on the

water with my Jesus.

My foot is on his neck,

and my joy is complete,

'cuz I'm dancing on the water

with my Jesus.

BRIDGE 3:

I am dancing. I am dancing.

I am dancing with my Lord.

I am dancing. I am dancing.

I am dancing – sweet romance.

CHORUS 2:

We don't wanna' stay here safe in the boat.

We wanna' dance on the

water with our Jesus.

We don't wanna' stay here safe in the boat.

We wanna' dance on the

water with our Jesus.

BRIDGE 2:

Bid us come, Lord. Bid us come, Lord.

Bid us come, Lord, dance with You.

Bid us come, Lord. Bid us come, Lord.

Bid us come, Lord, dance with You.

VERSE 2:

Satan is a liar, and he's under our feet,

'cuz we're dancing on the

water with our Jesus.

Our foot is on his neck,

and our joy is complete,

'cuz we're dancing on

the water with our Jesus.

BRIDGE 3:

We are dancing. We are dancing.

We are dancing with our Lord.

We are dancing. We are dancing.

We are dancing – sweet romance.

 BRIDGE 4:

Come and join us. Come and join us.

Come and join us in the dance.

Come and join us. Come and join us.

Come and join us – sweet romance.

ALL – SLOWLY with Emphasis

I don't wanna' stay here safe in the boat.

I wanna' walk on the water

with my Jesus.

Just Consider it Done

By Elizabeth C. (Betsy) Tice

THE INSPIRATION

Mark 16:1- 4 And when the sabbath was past, Mary Magdalene, and Mary the *mother* of James, and Salome, had bought sweet spices, that they might come and anoint him. 2 And very early in the morning the first *day* of the week, they came unto the sepulchre at the rising of the sun. 3 And they said among themselves, Who shall roll us away the stone from the door of the sepulchre? 4 And when they looked, they saw that the stone was rolled away: for it was very great.

Philippians 4:6 – 8 Be careful for nothing; but in every thing by prayer and supplication with thanksgiving let your requests be made known unto God. 7 And the peace of God, which passeth all understanding, shall keep your hearts and minds through Christ Jesus. 8 Finally, brethren, whatsoever things are true, whatsoever things *are* honest, whatsoever things *are* just, whatsoever things *are* pure, whatsoever things *are* lovely, whatsoever things *are* of good report; if *there be* any virtue, and if *there be* any praise, think on these things.

Hebrews 11:1 Now faith is the substance of things hoped for, the evidence of things not seen.

Hebrews 12: 1 – 2 Wherefore seeing we also are compassed about with so great a cloud of witnesses, let us lay aside every weight, and the sin which doth so easily beset *us,* and let us run with patience the race that is set before us, 2 Looking unto Jesus the author and finisher of *our* faith; who for the joy that was set before him endured the ross, despising the shame, and is set down at the right hand of the throne of God.

Matthew 17:20 -21 And Jesus said unto them, Because of your unbelief: for verily I say unto you, If ye have faith as a grain of mustard seed, ye shall say unto this mountain, Remove hence to yonder place; and it shall remove; and nothing shall be impossible unto you. 21 Howbeit this kind goeth not out but by prayer and fasting.

Just Consider it Done

********** SONG **********

By Elizabeth C. (Betsy) Tice

(Mark 16:1- 4, Philippians 4:6 - 8, Hebrews 11:1 and 12: 1 – 2, and Matthew 17:20 -21)

Worry, worry, worry worry. Worry, worry, worry, worry. (Repeat)

Fret, fret, fret, fret. Fret, fret, fret, fret.

(Repeat)

STOP! JUST STOP!

CHORUS:

Just consider it done.

(5 claps, the 1st with done)

Just consider it done.

(8 *claps, the 1st with done*)

Faith will move the mountain

when I just consider it done.

Just consider it done.
(5 claps, the 1st with done)
Just consider it done.
(8 claps, the 1st with done)
Faith will move the mountain
when I just consider it done.

VERSE 1:
I'll consider it done.
(5 claps, the 1st with done)
I'll consider it done.
(8 claps, the 1st with done)
Faith will move the mountain
when I just consider it done.
I'll consider it done.
(5 claps, the 1st with done)
I'll consider it done.

(8 *claps, the 1st with done*)
God will move the mountain
when I just consider it done.
VERSE 2:
I considered it done.
(5 claps, the 1st with done)
I considered it done.
(8 *claps, the 1st with done*)
Faith removed the mountain
when I just considered it done.
I considered it done.
(5 claps, the 1st with done)
I considered it done.
(8 *claps, the 1st with done*)
Jesus moved the mountain,
when I just considered it done.

Shake Off the Dust of Rejection

By Elizabeth C. (Betsy) Tice

THE INSPIRATION

Isaiah 53:3 -5 (KJV)

3 He is despised and rejected of men; a man of sorrows, and acquainted with grief: and we hid as it were our faces from him; he was despised, and we esteemed him not. 4 Surely he hath borne our griefs, and carried our sorrows: yet we did esteem him stricken, smitten of God, and afflicted. 5 But he was wounded for our transgressions, he was bruised for our iniquities: the chastisement of our peace was upon him; and with his stripes we are healed.

Matthew 10:11-15 And into whatsoever city or town ye shall enter, enquire who in it is worthy; and there abide till ye go thence. 12 And when ye come into an house, salute it. 13 And if the house be worthy, let your peace come upon it: but if it be not worthy, let your peace return to you. 14 And whosoever shall not receive you, nor hear your words, when ye depart out of that house or city, shake off the dust of your feet. 15 Verily I say unto you, It shall be more tolerable for the land of Sodom and Gomorrha in the day of judgment, than for that city.

Hebrews 12:1-2 Wherefore seeing we also are compassed about with so great a cloud of witnesses, let us lay aside every weight, and the sin which doth so easily beset *us,* and let us run with patience the race that is set before us, 2 Looking unto Jesus the author and finisher of *our* faith; who for the joy that was set before him endured the cross, despising the shame, and is set down at the right hand of the throne of God.

Revelation 2:17 He that hath an ear, let him hear what the Spirit saith unto the churches; To him that overcometh will I give to eat of the hidden manna, and will give him a white stone, and in the stone a new name written, which no man knoweth saving he that receiveth *it*.

Shake Off the
Dust of Rejection

********** SONG **********

By Elizabeth C. (Betsy) Tice

(Matthew 10:11-15, Isaiah 53, Hebrews 12:1-2, and Revelation 2:17)

CHORUS:

Shake off the dust of rejection

And seek the approval of God.

Our Lord, so despised, by men crucified,

Sits in Heaven, exalted on high.

VERSE 1:

Lay aside the weight of rejection.

The weight is too heavy to bear.

So run your race, looking to His face,

And you'll meet Him one day in the air.

VERSE 2:

When you have overcome,

You'll sit with Him in His throne.

You'll receive a new name and

a precious white stone;

And He'll tell heaven you are His own.

CHORUS:

Shake off the dust of rejection

And seek the approval of God.

Our Lord, so despised, by men crucified,

Sits in Heaven, exalted on high.

Let the Peace of God Rule in Your Heart

By Elizabeth C. (Betsy) Tice

THE INSPIRATION

Colossians 3:1-17 (With emphasis on 3:15) If ye then be risen with Christ, seek those things which are above, where Christ sitteth on the right hand of God. 2 Set your affection on things above, not on things on the earth. 3 For ye are dead, and your life is hid with Christ in God. 4 When Christ, *who is* our life, shall appear, then shall ye also appear with him in glory. 5 Mortify therefore your members which are upon the earth; fornication, uncleanness, inordinate affection, evil concupiscence, and covetousness, which is idolatry: 6 For which things' sake the wrath of God cometh on the children of disobedience: 7 In the which ye also walked some time, when ye lived in them. 8 But now ye also put off all these; anger, wrath, malice, blasphemy, filthy communication out of your mouth. 9 Lie not one to another, seeing that ye have put off the old man with his deeds; 10 And have put on the new *man,* which is renewed in knowledge after the image of him that created him: 11 Where there is neither Greek nor Jew, circumcision nor uncircumcision, Barbarian, Scythian, bond *nor* free: but Christ *is* all, and in all. 12 Put on therefore, as the elect of God, holy and beloved, bowels of mercies, kindness, humbleness of mind, meekness, longsuffering; 13 Forbearing one another, and forgiving one another, if any man have a quarrel against any: even as Christ forgave you, so also *do* ye. 14 And above all these things *put on* charity, which is the bond of perfectness. 15 And let the peace of God rule in your hearts, to the which also ye are called in one body; and be ye thankful. 16 Let the word of Christ dwell in you richly in all wisdom; teaching and admonishing one another in psalms and hymns and spiritual songs, singing with grace in your hearts to the Lord. 17 And whatsoever ye do in word or deed, *do* all in the name of the Lord Jesus, giving thanks to God and the Father by him.

John 14:27 Peace I leave with you, my peace I give unto you: not as the world giveth, give I unto you. Let not your heart be troubled, neither let it be afraid.

Let the Peace of God Rule in Your Heart

********** SONG **********

By Elizabeth C. (Betsy) Tice

(Colossians 3:15 KJV)

CHORUS: (Sing Two Times)

Let the peace of God rule in your heart.

Let the peace of God rule in your heart,

And be ye thankful. Be ye thankful,

And be ye thankful

For all things.

In Your Presence, O God

By Elizabeth C. Betsy)Tice

THE INSPIRATION

Psalm 91 He that dwelleth in the secret place of the most High shall abide under the shadow of the Almighty. 2 I will say of the LORD, *He is* my refuge and my fortress: my God; in him will I trust. 3 Surely he shall deliver thee from the snare of the fowler, *and* from the noisome pestilence. 4 He shall cover thee with his feathers, and under his wings shalt thou trust: his truth *shall be thy* shield and buckler. 5 Thou shalt not be afraid for the terror by night; *nor* for the arrow *that* flieth by day; 6 *Nor* for the pestilence *that* walketh in darkness; *nor* for the destruction *that* wasteth at noonday. 7 A thousand shall fall at thy side, and ten thousand at thy right hand; *but* it shall not come nigh thee. 8 Only with thine eyes shalt thou behold and see the reward of the wicked. 9 Because thou hast made the LORD, *which is* my refuge, *even* the most High, thy habitation; 10 There shall no evil befall thee, neither shall any plague come nigh thy dwelling. 11 For he shall give his angels charge over thee, to keep thee in all thy ways. 12 They shall bear thee up in *their* hands, lest thou dash thy foot against a stone. 13 Thou shalt tread upon the lion and adder: the young lion and the dragon shalt thou trample under feet. 14 Because he hath set his love upon me, therefore will I deliver him: I will set him on high, because he hath known my name. 15 He shall call upon me, and I will answer him: I *will be* with him in trouble; I will deliver him, and honour him. 16 With long life will I satisfy him, and shew him my salvation.

Psalm 119:9-16 Wherewithal shall a young man cleanse his way? by taking heed *thereto* according to thy word. 10 With my whole heart have I sought thee: O let me not wander from thy commandments. 11 Thy word have I hid in mine heart, that I might not sin against thee. 12 Blessed *art* thou, O LORD: teach me thy statutes. 13 With my lips have I declared all the judgments of thy mouth. 14 I have rejoiced in the way of thy testimonies, as *much as* in all riches. 15 I will meditate in thy precepts, and have respect unto thy ways. 16 I will delight myself in thy statutes: I will not forget thy word.

Proverbs 18:24 A man *that hath* friends must shew himself friendly: and there is a friend *that* sticketh closer than a brother.

In Your Presence, O God

********** SONG **********

By Elizabeth C. (Betsy) Tice

(Psalms 91 and 119, and Proverbs 18:24)

VERSE 1:

In Your presence, O God, there is healing.

In Your presence, O God, sweet release.

In Your presence, O Lord,

there is joy without end.

In Your presence, O Lord,

there is peace.

CHORUS:

Let me dwell in Your presence, O Lord.

Let me worship and learn at Your feet.

Let me look on Your face

and be lost in Your grace.

Let me dwell in Your presence, O Lord.
VERSE 2:
There are friends here on Earth,
whom we cherish,
And their love brings such joy to our heart.
Yet the greatest of all of life's treasures
Is the Friend Who will never depart.
CHORUS:
Let me dwell in Your presence, O Lord.
Let me worship and learn at Your feet.
Let me look on Your face and
be lost in Your grace.
Let me dwell in Your presence, O Lord.

Seek My Face

By Elizabeth C. (Betsy) Tice

THE INSPIRATION

Psalm 27:8 When thou saidst, Seek ye my face; my heart said unto thee, Thy face, LORD, will I seek.

Acts 1-2:4 The former treatise have I made, O Theophilus, of all that Jesus began both to do and teach, 2 Until the day in which he was taken up, after that he through the Holy Ghost had given commandments unto the apostles whom he had chosen: 3 To whom also he shewed himself alive after his passion by many infallible proofs, being seen of them forty days, and speaking of the things pertaining to the kingdom of God: 4 And, being assembled together with *them,* commanded them that they should not depart from Jerusalem, but wait for the promise of the Father, which, *saith he,* ye have heard of me. 5 For John truly baptized with water; but ye shall be baptized with the Holy Ghost not many days hence. 6 When they therefore were come together, they asked of him, saying, Lord, wilt thou at this time restore again the kingdom to Israel? 7 And he said unto them, It is not for you to know the times or the seasons, which the Father hath put in his own power. 8 But ye shall receive power, after that the Holy Ghost is come upon you: and ye shall be witnesses unto me both in Jerusalem, and in all Judaea, and in Samaria, and unto the uttermost part of the earth. 9 And when he had spoken these things, while they beheld, he was taken up; and a cloud received him out of their sight. 10 And while they looked stedfastly toward heaven as he went up, behold, two men stood by them in white apparel; 11 Which also said, Ye men of

Galilee, why stand ye gazing up into heaven? this same Jesus, which is taken up from you into heaven, shall so come in like manner as ye have seen him go into heaven. 12 Then returned they unto Jerusalem from the mount called Olivet, which is from Jerusalem a sabbath day's journey. 13 And when they were come in, they went up into an upper room, where abode both Peter, and James, and John, and Andrew, Philip, and Thomas, Bartholomew, and Matthew, James *the son* of Alphaeus, and Simon Zelotes, and Judas *the brother* of James. 14 These all continued with one accord in prayer and supplication, with the women, and Mary the mother of Jesus, and with his brethren. 15 And in those days Peter stood up in the midst of the disciples, and said, (the number of names together were about an hundred and twenty,) 16 Men *and* brethren, this scripture must needs have been fulfilled, which the Holy Ghost by the mouth of David spake before concerning Judas, which was guide to them that took Jesus. 17 For he was numbered with us, and had obtained part of this ministry. 18 Now this man purchased a field with the reward of iniquity; and falling headlong, he burst asunder in the midst, and all his bowels gushed out. 19 And it was known unto all the dwellers at Jerusalem; insomuch as that field is called in their proper tongue, Aceldama, that is to say, The field of blood. 20 For it is written in the book of Psalms, Let his habitation be desolate, and let no man dwell therein: and his bishoprick let another take. 21 Wherefore of these men which have companied with us all the time that the Lord Jesus went in and out among us, 22 Beginning from the baptism of John, unto that same day that he was taken up from us, must one be ordained to be a witness with us of his resurrection. 23 And they appointed two, Joseph called Barsabas, who was surnamed Justus, and Matthias. 24 And they prayed, and said, Thou, Lord, which knowest the hearts of all *men,* shew whether of these two thou hast chosen, 25 That he may take part of this ministry and apostleship, from which Judas by transgression fell, that he might go to his own place. 26 And they gave forth their lots; and the lot fell upon Matthias; and he was numbered with the eleven apostles.

Acts 2:1 And when the day of Pentecost was fully come, they were all with one accord in one place. 2 And suddenly there came a sound from heaven as of a rushing mighty wind, and it filled all the house where they were sitting. 3 And there appeared unto them cloven tongues like as of fire, and it sat upon each of them. 4 And they were all filled with the Holy Ghost, and began to speak with other tongues, as the Spirit gave them utterance.

Seek My Face

********** SONG **********

By Elizabeth C. (Betsy) Tice
(Psalm 27:8 and Acts 1-2:4)

CHORUS:

"Seek My face. Seek My face

If you would partake of My grace.

Seek My face. Seek My face.

The answer will come

when you seek My face."

VERSE 1:

"He is gone," His disciples said,

"Though we know He rose from the dead."

"Now we're alone. What shall we do?"

"Wait, and My Spirit will come to you."
CHORUS:
"Seek My face. Seek My face
If you would partake of My grace.
Seek My face. Seek My face.
The answer will come
when you seek My face."
VERSE 2:
So they prayed in unity,
Trusting that soon His promise they'd see.
And when the time to receive had come,
Then came the Spirit with cloven tongues.
CHORUS:
"Seek My face. Seek My face
If you would partake of My grace.
Seek My face. Seek My face.
The answer will come when

you seek My face."
VERSE 3:
Friend, have you reached
the depths of despair,
Thinking that no one is left to care.
Turn to the One who died for you.
There is no limit to what He will do
CHORUS:
"Seek My face. Seek My face
If you would partake of My grace.
Seek My face. Seek My face.
The answer will come
when you seek My face."

We Are Changed
From Glory to Glory

By Elizabeth C. (Betsy) Tice

THE INSPIRATION

2 Corinthians 3:18 But we all, with open face beholding as in a glass the glory of the Lord, are changed into the same image from glory to glory, *even* as by the Spirit of the Lord.

Psalm 16:11 Thou wilt shew me the path of life: in thy presence is fulness of joy; at thy right hand there are pleasures for evermore.

Exodus 33:14 And he said, My presence

shall go with thee, and I will give thee rest.

Psalm 27:8 When thou saidst, Seek ye my face; my heart said unto thee, Thy face, LORD, will I seek.

Jeremiah 29:13 And ye shall seek me, and find me, when ye shall search for me with all your heart.

John 14:26 But the Comforter, which is the Holy Ghost, whom the Father will send in my name, he shall teach you all things, and bring all things to your remembrance, whatsoever I have said unto you.

Psalm 145:18 The LORD is nigh unto all them that call upon him, to all that call upon him in truth.

Matthew 5:8 Blessed are the pure in heart: for they shall see God.

Hebrews 13:5 Let your conversation be without covetousness; and be content with such things as ye have: for he hath said, I will never leave thee, nor forsake thee.

Revelation 3:20 Behold, I stand at the door, and knock: if any man hear my voice, and open the door, I will come in to him, and will sup with him, and he with me.

Hebrews 4:16 Let us therefore come boldly unto the throne of grace, that we may obtain mercy, and find grace to help in time of need.

Acts 17:27 That they should seek the Lord, if haply they might feel after him, and find him, though he be not far from every one of us:

2 Peter 3:9 The Lord is not slack concerning his promise, as some men count slackness; but is longsuffering to us-ward, not willing that any should perish, but that all should come to repentance.

Isaiah 60:1 Arise, shine; for thy light is come, and the glory of the LORD is risen upon thee.

We Are Changed
From Glory to Glory

********** SONG **********

By Elizabeth C. (Betsy) Tice

(II Corinthians 3:18 KJV)

CHORUS:

We are changed from glory to glory,

As we look into Your face,

And the world no longer holds us

As we sing, "Amazing Grace."

VERSE 1:

We are feasting at Your table.

We are sheltered in Your arms.

And though satan's wrath still rages,

We are safe from all alarms.

VERSE 2:

We abide beneath Your shadow.

We dwell in Your secret place.

There no evil foe can harm us

As we gaze upon Your face.

VERSE 3:

We have cast our cares on Jesus.

We are resting in His love.

Oh, the joy within His presence,

Seated with our Lord above.

CHORUS:

We are changed from glory to glory,

As we look into Your face,

And the world no longer holds us

As we sing, "Amazing Grace."

BOOKS
**You may find all our books at:
Ticehouse.com**

Elizabeth C. (Betsy) Tice
My Heart Sings Out to Jesus
Living Life in Your Parallel Universe
To Live in His Love – Loving Each Other
To Live in His Love – I Live to Please Him

Orvil L. (Ty) Tice
Counseling through the Gifts of the Holy Spirit
Unboxing Your Calling
Spirits Over The Valley

COAUTHORS - Betsy & Ty Tice
THE POWER OF THE SUPERNATURAL
Return to the Book of Acts

FREE EBOOK – GOD CALLS YOU
SPECIAL
REQUEST IT AT: tyandbetsy@gmail.com

Valid links as of 7/11/2025

Ty and Betsy Tice's Facebook Pages, Webpage, Podbean

https://www.facebook.com/bishopty.tice
https://www.facebook.com/betsy.tice

Web Page https://www.ticehouse.com
Podbean https://bishoptice.podbean.com

Ty's YouTube Channel
In your You Tube search bar
type in
@bishoptyandbetsytice

Betsy's You Tube Channel
In your You Tube search bar
type in
@betsyssongsfromtheholyspir4592